The Felon's 2019 Guide to Finding a Job & Becoming an Entrepreneur
Copyright 2018 by Prison Rideshare Network
Researched and Written by Toyo Bukhari
Edited by Daniel Acosta
Co-Researched, Co-Authored and Co-Edited by Kiesha Joseph
Published by Prison Rideshare Network

All rights reserved. Without limiting the rights under the copyright reserved above, no part of this publication may be reproduced, stored in, or introduced into a retrieval system, or transmitted in any form or by any means (electronic, mechanical, photocopying, recording, or otherwise) without prior written permission.

For permission requests, please contact: info@prisonrideshare.org

Thank you for downloading this eBook. It remains the copyrighted property of Prison Rideshare Network and may not be reproduced, copied or distributed for any commercial or non-commercial purposes.

If you enjoyed this book, please encourage your friends to download their own copy at prisonrideshare.org. Thank you for your support and respect for the property of this author and publisher.

Printed in the USA

eBook ASIN: B07KJHVZT2
Paperback ISBN: 9781790148455

Table of Contents

Foreword 6
Acknowledgements 7
Introduction 8
Need Help Getting a Job After Prison? Help Is Here! 9
4 Steps to Landing a Job as an Ex-Convict 10
    1. Get Work Experience 10
    2. Prepare Your Resume 10
    3. Reach Out & Submit Job Applications 11
    4. Keep Your Downtime After Prison Productive and Busy 11
Tips for Applying for Jobs After Prison 12
    Organizing Your Job Search Efforts 12
    10 Easy Ways to Organize Your Job Search 12
Functional Resume Tips for the Ex-Prisoners 14
    Reasons for Using a Functional Resume VS Chronological 14
    How to Create a Functional Resume 14
    5 Steps to Creating a Cover Letter for Your Resume 16
    Things to Consider When Interviewing for a Job as a Felon 18
Job Interview Hacks to Help the Formerly Incarcerated Get Jobs After Prison 20
    3 Job Interview Tips for Former Convicts 20
How to Answer Common Tricky Questions Potential Employers Ask Ex-Prisoners 24
    6 Common Questions Interviewers Ask Felons Looking for Jobs 24
    Example Interview Answers for Ex-Convicts Hunting for Jobs 25
    Interview Questions Potential Employers Are NOT Allowed to Ask 25
    What If a Potential Employer Asks a Questionable Question? 26
    Prepare a Felony Letter of Explanation 27
Background Checks for Ex-Prisoners Looking for Jobs 30
    Run a Criminal Background Check on Yourself Before the Interview 30
    Get Your Credit Reports and Scores After Prison 30
5 Job Opportunity Sources, Directories & Support Systems for Ex-Convicts 32
    1. Non-Profit Organizations 32
    2. Center for Employment Opportunities 32

3. Safer Foundation 33
4. Project RIO 33
5. Other Agencies That Assist with Ex-Con Employment and/or Training .. 34

Government & Local Job Portals That Help Former Prisoners 35

Jobs for Ex-Convicts: Official Employment Portals for Each State in The U.S. 35

State Agency's Employment Portals 36
Private Job Portals 36

Top 100 Employers Who Hire Ex-Prisoners in the U.S. 38

100 Jobs That Tend to Hire Felons 38

Entrepreneurship: Looking Beyond Paid Employment for Ex-Prisoners 42

Entrepreneurship for Felons 42
4 Tips for Getting Resources to Start Your Own Business 42
Entrepreneurship: Do Your Due Diligence First 44

Lucrative Business Ideas for the Ex-Convict Entrepreneur 45

Service Areas 45
Production Niches 45
Freelance Gigs 46
Entrepreneurship Isn't for All Former Prisoners 46

How to Get Credit for Your Business as an Ex-Convict 47

Top 10 Avenues to Get Small Business Grants for the Formerly Incarcerated 48
Get Help Establishing Personal Credit 52
Get Help Establishing Business Credit 53

About Prison Rideshare Network 54

Engage with Us Online 54

Foreword

I am **Kiesha Joseph**, a published author, content manager, Editor-in-Chief and prison loved one. When **Toyo Bukhari** approached me about creating a few blog posts to help ex-convicts find jobs after prison, it sounded like an awesome idea to me. My mother was due to be released from CIW in a matter of months. She and I could both use information like this to get her on her feet.

By the time Toyo began his research, he had already been a virtual assistant for the **Prison Rideshare Network (PRN)** brand for about a year. He had spent all of this time searching for hot prison news stories, researching topics, editing content and working as my "left-hand man." So, I had no doubt that he knew exactly what type of information our audience needs.

Toyo submitted articles related to helping felons find jobs. And, to my surprise, he also included well-thought-out content to guide ex-prisoners through the process of finding business opportunities and launching and growing new startups. He included so much useful content that there was no way we could waste it on simple blog posts.

I decided to transform his pieces into an eBook. That's when the idea behind **The Felon's 2019 Guide to Finding a Job & Becoming an Entrepreneur** was born.

My Editor-in-Training, **Daniel Acosta**, turned the posts into an eBook, completing the basic visual formatting. He also added his SEO-editing touches, based on his extensive training as a **Content Marketing Geek**. This helped create an engaging, interactive guide for felons eBook.

With much more extensive research, content writing and visual editing, I was able to transform the simple eBook into an informative, comprehensive book with step-by-step instructions, tips and tricks for finding jobs and starting small businesses after prison.

As a prison daughter, sister, cousin and friend, I know what our loved ones need when they get out of prisons. One of the most important needs that can be hard to fulfill are long-term, decent-paying jobs. Helping newly released prison inmates find jobs leads to lower recidivism rates, which puts a dent in mass incarceration.

This paperback book publication is Prison Rideshare Network's effort to do our part to help felons find jobs that can actually support them after they get out. As the owner of PRN, I truly hope it brings value to the lives of our audience.

I dedicate this publication to my mother, **Audrey Chatmon** #X22166.

Signed,
Kiesha Joseph
Compton, CA
Tuesday, November 20, 2018

Acknowledgements

The team behind Prison Rideshare Network has been working hard to build traffic and create valuable content for our audience. We have spent the past year going through many ups-and-downs, from website viruses to locked bank accounts, from vindictive writers to implementing new processes... we've endured and stood strong.

Some of our virtual assistants, editors, writers and data entry stars have been with us since the beginning and still remain on the team to this day. Others have gone on to do other things, with two "right-hand women" even going on to work in other countries.

I would like to acknowledge and give thanks to the following Prison Rideshare Network team members for their hard work and commitment to the brand:

- Abigael Shem
- Charles Omedo
- Daniel Acosta
- Heather Kay
- Heidi Smith
- Joseph Ogolla
- Kiesha Joseph
- Latoya Taylor
- Merri Wong
- Nicholas Sweeney
- Toyo Bukhari
- Riley Wharton
- Shantoya Taylor
- Tami Dixon
- Tina Karen

Introduction

Prison Rideshare Network is a nonprofit organization. We produced this comprehensive guide as a tool to help formerly incarcerated people. Our goal is to help you thrive financially through gainful employment and/or entrepreneurship after your prison release.

This guide to employment and entrepreneurship includes useful information to help you find jobs with companies that hire felons. We offer tips to help you create your resume and cover letter, as well as get through the interview process and background checks, which can be very intimidating for ex-cons.

You'll find useful tips on starting your own business. Get ideas for type of businesses you can launch, even if you're on parole. Learn how to find small business funding and establishing both personal and business to become a successful entrepreneur.

The Felon's 2019 Guide to Finding a Job & Becoming an Entrepreneur is a useful tool for anyone currently or formerly incarcerated with a felony record. Don't let your past dictate your future. You can still achieve your financial goals, even if you've served prison time.

Need Help Getting a Job After Prison? Help Is Here!

Getting a job is undeniably difficult for a felon. However, as bad as it seems, there are still great employment opportunities to land a decent job, even if you've done prison time.

About 6.9 million people have been convicted of crimes within the U.S. justice system. That is an alarming number, which is why many believe mass incarceration is such an issue in this country.

As time goes on, society has become steadily more receptive to reintegrating formerly incarcerated people. Those pushing increasingly further for these ex-convicts include:

- Volunteer groups
- Government job directories
- Progressive 21st century companies

They are at the forefront of reintroducing ex-convicts into the labor market.

4 Steps to Landing a Job as an Ex-Convict

If you're on parole or probation, your PO (parole officer or probation officer) more than likely requires that you find gainful employment in order to remain free. Even if you're not on probation or parole, you still need a job to become a productive member of society.

Here are four steps to help you get hired after your prison release:

1. Get Work Experience

Gathering work experience is important in order to qualify for most ideal employment opportunities. It's almost impossible to land a dream job immediately upon release from prison. This is because it's likely the only recent experience you have (if any at all) is prison job experience.

Whatever job or career path you intend to pursue after prison, try to find volunteer work or a low wage job in the field your field of interest. This helps build your credentials and competency for your dream job in the future.

We'll discuss agencies that help ex-convicts find job openings later in this eBook.

2. Prepare Your Resume

Volunteer agencies who help formerly incarcerated inmates find jobs usually offer professional resume writing services as well. If you are creating your resume yourself, don't state that you've been formerly incarcerated.

Only mention it if (and ONLY IF) the job posting requires you to do so directly on your resume.

Also, don't arrange your work experience in chronological order. List them in order of relevance to the job you're applying for instead.

This little resume hack will make your inactive labor years less evident. Remember, you don't have any recent, appealing job experience. You need to find creative ways to make sure this doesn't stand out, at least until you get that invitation to interview for a job.

We will go into more detail about creating a functional resume that allows an ex-inmate to shine.

3. Reach Out & Submit Job Applications

The truth is, you may get turned down a lot simply because of your criminal record and prison time. Even applicants who haven't been incarcerated get turned down a lot in the current job market.

However, you have to keep at it. According to Business Insider, one former prisoner submitted many job applications before he got an ideal job placement.

Don't be discouraged by rejections. If you are eligible and interested, go ahead and apply. You'll be surprised how many companies will hire an ex-con if the candidate has the qualifications and attitude they're looking for overall.

4. Keep Your Downtime After Prison Productive and Busy

They say idle hands are the devil's workshop. It's important to stay productive during the space of your job hunt. The last thing you want is to rack up even more idle time on your resume.

Instead, you can:

- Volunteer
- Learn a skill hands-on
- Further your education
- Read some books to learn new skills

All of these job-related activities are valuable pieces of information to add to your resume. They show that you've been busy, and not just sitting around doing nothing while hunting for a job after release.

You don't have to be restricted to these choices. Just avoid becoming idle. It isn't helpful to your peace of mind while you search.

Tips for Applying for Jobs After Prison

Once again, you don't want idle time on your hands once you get your freedom. Make it a point to do something productive each and every day to improve your lifestyle more and more overtime.

Here are some tips to help you with your after prison job search:

- **Improve yourself constantly:** This may include picking a short training program to help broaden or sharpen your knowledge base.
- **KISS (Keep It Simple and Short):** Except if you're asked or feel the need to share, keep quiet. This applies to writing your CV and during interviews.
- **Don't get tired of applying:** Who doesn't get rejected? Rejection shouldn't fizzle you out. Respond to all rejections positively by improving your weaknesses and trying again.
- **Give your all:** Some companies hire with a probationary period. Others place potential staff on specific paid training. Either way, always work hard and conduct yourself the best that you can.

Organizing Your Job Search Efforts

During your job search, you may find yourself submitting multiple applications, both online and in-person. This involves a lot of time, giving you a lot to track. You need to keep up with application deadlines, app statuses, interview processes and times and especially follow-up opportunities.

So, it's important that you keep track of your apps. This allows you to stay organized, so no opportunities go misses.

Many people use simple Word docs and Excel spreadsheets. Then, they create reminder systems to keep them on top of any and all opportunities to follow-up with prospects. There, they record conversation notes and keep track of applications, as well as job interviews.

There are also some very effective online tools you can use to track your jobs searches and interviews. They are much better at managing your job searches and helping you identity potential job opportunities. This is very important for someone fresh out whose simply not very computer savvy.

10 Easy Ways to Organize Your Job Search

The Balance Careers has published a list of 10 simple ways for you to create databases and sheets to keep your job applications organized. Check it out here: https://www.thebalancecareers.com/organize-your-job-search-2060710

Here at Prison Rideshare Network, we use Airtable to organize everything from applicants and team members to content management and tasks. Airtable is essentially much like Excel, but it uses modern technology to make it much more user-friendly.

Using Airtable, you can create your own bases (spreadsheets) from scratch to track your job hunting progress... **for FREE**! There are also some very useful templates created specifically for helping you stay organized while you hunt for a job.

The Airtable template below is called **Job Hunting**. It already has the fields you need to organize your job search. This FREE template helps you keep track of job openings, applications, interviews, answers to your interview questions and more.

It's user-friendly, free and extremely mobile friendly. Access your bases via Airtable.com using any mobile device. Or, simply download the mobile app and you're ready to go!

Interested in using this free tool for job hunting tracking? Simply create your FREE account and look for the **Job Hunting Template**.

Sign up for a FREE Airtable here: https://airtable.com/invite/r/Vb77G1iX

Functional Resume Tips for the Ex-Prisoners

The most common type of resume the chronological resume. This is when you simply list a timeline of your work experience in reverse order. Chronological resumes cause recruiters to focus on the job titles and how much time you've spent utilizing your skills.

These resumes also cause potential employers to focus on how much time you've spent *unemployed*. And, since you've spent some time in prison, you more than likely have large gaps in your employment history.

Reasons for Using a Functional Resume VS Chronological

Functional resumes focus on your experience and skills instead. They put emphasis on specific capabilities and skills to highlight your true abilities as an employee.

So, why should you use a functional resume instead of a chronological one after doing time in prison? Here are some of the main reasons people go with this format:

- Have changed jobs frequently
- Transitioning into a new field
- Possess "out-of-the-box" skills
- Are reentering the workforce
- Have gaps in their work history

As someone who has done time, you will probably have major gaps in your work history. You're definitely trying to get back into the workforce. And, if you've had jobs in prisons over the years, your skills are quite "out-of-the-box," which may or may not lead you to trying to get into a new field.

A functional resume brings attention to the transferable skills you've acquired while working. For example, let's say you managed the kitchen while in prison. In essence, you probably also managed the kitchen staff, training, and some inventory and stock.

How to Create a Functional Resume

Your resume is your chance to package yourself. Allow your skills to shine. That will increase your chances of landing a job interview. Here are some tips to help you get started:

1. Start with a Summary

Your resume summary statement should be just a few sentences or a brief list at the beginning of the resume, right after your contact information. Its purpose is to highlight the qualifications you possess for a particular job. The summary gives recruiters a brief rundown of your professional qualifications.

In your resume summary, make sure you include information that shows how you brought value to the jobs, teams or companies for which you've worked. Show how you were instrumental in transforming your departments. The hiring manager needs to feel like you would be an asset to the company.

The Balance Careers offers some great tips on how to write a resume summary with examples. Download a free resume template here: https://www.thebalancecareers.com/how-to-write-a-resume-summary-statement-2061034

2. Organize by Themes

Instead of listing your past job in reverse chronological order, organize it by themes. Your resume's themes may be qualifications or skills within the resume itself. For example, you may have had two main jobs: "Kitchen Management" and "Firefighting"

For a functional resume, you would group your jobs skills under these two categories. Group the skills together so potential employers can see that you possess the right skills for the job, at-a-glance. Under each category theme, list the job duties you carried out for that job.

That way, even if you're applying for a job as a package handler, related skills are showcased for the recruiter to see. Such skills may include things like management, working with teams, lifting heavy objects constantly, standing for long periods of time, etc...

3. Keywords Are Key

Keywords are essential when it comes to resumes. Make sure yours includes keywords related to your skills that are included in the job description. Add these important keywords to your titles or in bullet lists to describe your accomplishments and skills in detail.

Using keywords from the job description helps the potential employer see that your skills and abilities match with the requirements of the job.

4. Include Relevant Projects

If you've taken part in any other personal or professional projects that are related to the job. You want to show how much success you've had developing processes and tasks and completing them.

5. Provide Employment History

In the end, you still may need to include your job history. If so, add this to the end of the resume. That way, hiring managers put more focus on your skills, instead of the gaps in your work history.

6. Create a Strong Cover Letter

Write a strong cover letter to include with your functional resume. It needs to expand on the abilities and skills you possess that make you a good candidate for the job. That way, the recruiter is less concerned about the gaps in your employment history.

Functional Resume Sample - Image Source: Zety.com

5 Steps to Creating a Cover Letter for Your Resume

Your cover letter is a creative way of introducing yourself to the potential employer. It needs show how your skills can bring value to the company and the job itself. If the reader doesn't like your cover letter, chances are your resume will never get read.

Use these five steps to write a strong, winning resume:

1. Create Your Header

The header of your professional cover letter should always include the following:
- Your Name
- Your City & State
- Your Telephone Number
- Your Email Address
- The Date
- Hiring Manager's Name & Title (if known)
- Name and Address of Company Applying to for Employment

2. Open with a Greeting

Always try to address your cover letter to the hiring manager when possible. Make sure it catches the reader's attention with a personalized greeting that addresses the person by name.

If you don't have access to the person's name, simply use a title, such as "Dear Hiring Manager."

3. Read the Listing Carefully

Check out the job listing very carefully. Try to figure out where your own skills and experience match up best. Highlight the requirements you possess listed in the job post.

Make sure your cover letter is only one page long. Choose to highlight the points that are most relevant to the position. Also, include the ones the give the recruiter fascinating stories and specific examples related to your experience.

4. Write a Catchy Opening Paragraph

The first few sentences of your opening paragraph needs to be very catchy. This will determine whether or not the rest of your resume gets read. The first paragraph needs to immediately capture the attention of the recruiter to hold the person's interest.

In the second paragraph, let the firing manager know that you have what the company is seeking in an employee. Show how your skills and abilities satisfy the specific needs of the company.

Read "How to Start a Cover Letter: Sample & Complete Guide [20+ Examples]" at: https://zety.com/blog/how-to-write-a-cover-letter

5. Explain Why You Want the Job

If the company is looking for a new employee, then it has needs. Your goal is to make sure they know that you are the solution that are seeking.

Most employers are concerned with creating a positive job atmosphere. That means hiring people who actually enjoy working with the company. This is an indication that you will probably remain a loyal employer for a long period of time.

In your cover letter's third paragraph, show the potential employer why you want this job specifically. Here are three ideas for explaining why you would prefer this job over any other:

- Explain why you find the job so interesting
- Research the company and explain why you find the brand so fascinating
- Show how your knowledge and experience will add to the current project

6. End with a Follow-Up Promise

Give your cover letter a strong ending by promising a "next step" follow-up. This makes it easier for the recruiter to remember you.

That way, when you reach out to follow-up on your resume submission, it will trigger the memory of reading your cover letter. This will push them to want to retrieve it and the resume to look them over again.

Let the reader know that you look forward to an in-person meeting to discuss the position. Remind the hiring manager how your knowledge and experience can help the company fulfill future goals.

Read "Closing a Cover Letter" at: https://www.thebalancecareers.com/cover-letter-closing-examples-2060311

Things to Consider When Interviewing for a Job as a Felon

Honesty will always be your best policy. While you aren't required to disclose every detail of your life to your potential employers, it's in your best interest to answer what you're asked honestly (as long as it's a fair question).

Whether your answer to the question is a positive or negative one, you must be sure to convincingly sell your side of the story. Highlight concrete examples of how your past is behind you. Show that you've made changes in your life before and after incarceration.

Since you already have a criminal record, the last thing you want to do is commit a felony trying to get a job. Going back to prison adds to the country's recidivism rate. You'd definitely want to avoid being a part of those statistics after just getting out.

In order to prevent the worst, keep these tips in mind about lying to potential employers:

- If you lie on a federal government job application or a job that requires special qualifications, involves dealing with drugs (nursing, care or

paramedic) or requires you to carry a firearm, you'd be so lucky not to land in prison. **Be honest!**
- If you are released on parole and lie about your felony conviction status to your employer, what you would say if your parole officer shows up? This is a **violation** of your parole!

You have to do more than promise or plan to do better. Your cover letter and interviews are great ways to tell the potential employer the steps you have taken towards creating a new life. Make yourself shine in spite of your past on your resume. And, you'll increase your chances of landing a job.

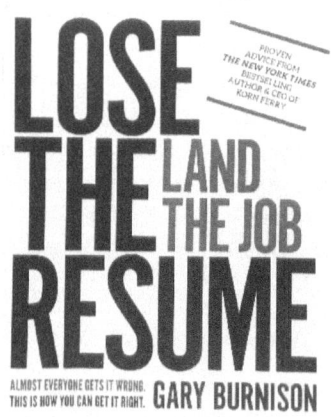

Need more assistance writing your functional resume? The book entitled **Loss the Resume, Land the Job** will help you learn how to tell your story and land a job interview. Click the image below for details.

Check it out here: https://amzn.to/2ONa8d2

Job Interview Hacks to Help the Formerly Incarcerated Get Jobs After Prison

Are you an ex-convict actively looking for a job? Well, we have some effective tips to help you get through the interview process, so you can land **employment after incarceration.**

Blindly sending out resumes in the hopes someone will respond is a waste of time and a big mistake for the formerly incarcerated. While some resumes make it to the shredder, some never even get read and end up in the garbage.

Employers don't usually hire people based solely on a great descriptive resume. The interview process is where most ex-felons are taken to task. But, with the right information and preparation. You stand a better chance at landing the job.

3 Job Interview Tips for Former Convicts

Interviewing for a job is hard enough. But, when your background includes prison time, interviews can be very intimidating. Yet, they don't have to be, even for ex-inmates.

Here are three tips to help felons get through the job interview process with calmness and confidence:

1. Your Appearance as an Ex-Convict is Everything

Unfortunately, a person is often judged by how they dress. If you have a criminal record, you need as much positivity as you can gather. There is already a big dent on your record.

A modest appearance gives the interviewer a good first impression. It also sends a subtle message of confidence.

You don't want to look too exotic and flashy. Instead, go with basic and elegant. Your job interview dress attire doesn't have to be new or expensive. It should be well ironed and neat enough to meet Mr. President at the White House.

When deciding what to wear to your job interview, keep the type of job in mind. For example, if you're interviewing for a warehouse job, you wouldn't go dressed in an expensive 3-piece suit.

Why? Well, what if they want you to start today? Make sure you're neat and clean, but not so dressy that you're too clean to get to work today.

Just keep in mind the job for which you're applying. If it's a blue-collar job, dress business casual. But, make sure you look as if you came to get some work done.

2. Tattoos Are Employment Turn-Offs After Prison

Unless you are interviewing for a position of a DJ or tattoo artist, most employers won't be too impressed with tattoos. Prison tattoos can be an extra big dent in your appearance during job interviews.

People in the corporate world tend to pass judgment immediately when they see tattoos on people with criminal pasts. They stereotypically relate them to gangs, drugs and other such issues.

It is best and advisable to keep your street and prison tattoos covered. If they cannot be covered, it might be best to go through the expense and pain of getting your tattoos removed.

Video: How to Cover Prison Tattoos with Makeup for Your Job Interview

Depending on the job (and location of your tattoos) you may be seeking a less permanent and less expensive fix regarding your tattoos. Makeup is an effective, economical way to hide your tattoos temporarily.

For tips on using makeup to cover your tattoos before you go on a job interview, check out the YouTube video below here: https://youtu.be/sIHmZ0Ej43Y

3. Honesty Can Be Your Best Policy

Disclaimer: This isn't legal advice in any form. It's a conclusion based on the experience of the formerly incarcerated and general knowledge related to ex-convicts finding jobs.

There's nothing as soothing to the human conscience as telling the truth. Having nothing to hide contributes immensely to the confidence you have for yourself and others have in you.

While many people have gotten away with lies when looking for jobs, ex-cons included, you may not be so lucky if you attempt it. The consequences could be very harmful for your career and quite possibly your freedom.

However, lying on a job application or during an interview is only illegal in the case of perjury or fraud (remember, you actually sign documents certifying certain things). You aren't obligated to be transparent beyond what's required of you.

Is Honesty Truly the Best Policy for Ex-Convicts Looking for Jobs?

Let's say you manage to land a job interview and you're given a form to fill out. The first question just happens to be:

Have you been convicted of a felony in the past?

How do you answer?
You have three choices:

1. **Yes.** For them to ask the question, it means it's a factor in their decision. It may not be important to the job itself. However, once there is an equally competent candidate who answers no, you might lose the opportunity to get the job.
2. **No.** Before you tell a huge lie, think again. If it doesn't hurt you now, it might later. And that could be more disastrous in the long run. Many companies do criminal background checks, even before inviting you to interview. The background check may cover both state and federal agencies and is done for a 7-year span.
3. **Leave It Blank.** Leaving this line blank is as good as answering yes. The question is quite straightforward. Anything besides yes or no often means yes. When you choose not to answer the question at all, this can leave the interviewer with doubts. They'll think you definitely have something to hide.

Regardless of the answer, there are consequences. However, the safest answer might just be:
> **Yes, please ask for details during the oral interview.**

How to Answer Common Tricky Questions Potential Employers Ask Ex-Prisoners

If you land yourself a job interview, it means you are worthy of the position on your application and resume. The essence of an interview is to confirm whether you're as qualified in person as you are on paper.

During the course of a job interview, the interviewer will attempt to figure out possible areas where you fall short of the job. The conclusion of the interviewer will come from your appearance, persona and answers to the interview questions.

6 Common Questions Interviewers Ask Felons Looking for Jobs

Ex-convicts seeking jobs are subject to 'special' types of questions based on various reasons. Below is a list of common questions you are likely to face as a newly released prisoner:

1. **We discovered gaps in your work history. Please explain those gaps?** To avoid this question, avoid arranging your work experience in chronological order. That way, you don't bring immediate attention to any gaps in your job history.
2. **Have you been convicted of a felony in the past? Yes or No?** As discussed earlier, the safest answer may be, "*Yes, please ask for details during the oral interview.*" During the interview itself, highlight the changes and accomplishments you've made since your prison release.
3. **What were your convictions?** Give details about your conviction. Use positive and business statements only. Above all else, avoid negativity. However, be honest.
4. **What have you taken from the experience of doing time in a correctional facility?** Briefly highlight how you now see the world differently and more maturely. This is your time to show you've changed and have big plans for your future on the outside.
5. **How can we be assured that you won't commit the same crime?** Don't grovel, just reassure and re-emphasize you are a changed person. Highlight positive things you did in prison before your release, as well as any volunteer or community efforts you've accomplished after getting out.

6. **How much did you earn on your last job?** If your last job was in prison, earning less than $1 an hour, just answer, "minimum wage." Remember, keep it simple and short (KISS).

Example Interview Answers for Ex-Convicts Hunting for Jobs

Here's a good example of how you can respond to job interview questions related to your past criminal history and prison sentence:

I'm happy you asked. I understand the need for you to know about my past, to feel comfortable hiring me. It's not the most comfortable topic for me to discuss, but rest assured it had nothing to do with my past employers (If it had anything to do with your past employer, no need to say that).

At the lowest point in my past life, I was involved (or wrongly convicted) for XYZ. I agree that I should have done certain things differently. If only I could go the past and do so.

I have since taken time to learn and improve myself in all areas of my life. (State the things you have done to improve yourself) I have enrolled in a series of re-entry programs to better myself. (Remind them of those skills that make you a good fit for their organization).

I have enrolled in a series of clerical courses and can now type 55 WPM. I am also familiar with popular day-to-day business software programs. I took a crash course on customer management. I have excellent reception skills. I am passionate and dedicated to learning more about this industry. I strongly believe your organization will be ideal for my career.

Interview Questions Potential Employers Are NOT Allowed to Ask

Unless they are directly linked to the job itself, the following questions cannot be asked by potential employers:

- How old are you?
- Do you attend church?
- Are you married or where you?
- Tell us your sexual preference?
- How much do you weigh?
- Do you take drugs, drink, or both?
- Do you have children? If yes, how many? If yes, what about childcare?

- Do you belong to any political party?
- What is your height?
- Are you dating anyone?
- Would you mind going out with me?
- Do you have any obvious or hidden disability? If yes, tell us?
- Have you ever been arrested? If yes, what were the charges?
- Do you plan on having children or more than you have?
- Do you rent or own your home?
- Tell us about your health history.
- What does your spouse do?
- How much did you earn last year?
- What is your opinion on religion, social groups and politics?

Reasons Potential Employers May Ask Imposing Questions to Ex-Convicts

Some potential employers can trample on your rights and ask the questions anyway. However, they may or may not have good reasons for this, such as:

- The nature of the job requires it. For example, imagine the G.O.P. hiring a Democratic clerk.
- They can sense your hunger and they know you'd answer anything just to get the job.
- They may assume you are ignorant of labor law. Most people actually are, not just felons.
- The employer is ignorant of the law.

What If a Potential Employer Asks a Questionable Question?

In the event you are asked any illegal or uncomfortable question, you are subject to the following options:

- Answer the question. Depending on how unreasonable the question may be, you must use wisdom to judge whether or not this is a good option for you.
- Politely decline to answer the question, stating it is illegal or makes you uncomfortable.
- Switch the topic of discussion. Don't be rude. Be tactful about it.
- Make a light 'joke' around the question. Exercise caution here. **This can backfire.**

- Return the question with a deflective question: "Interesting, why do you ask?"
- Give a confused expression and ask: "I'm sorry, but does this question apply to the job?"
- Question the interviewer with: "If I decline to answer, does this disqualify me automatically?"
- Although discouraged, you can let the interviewer know what you think of the question: "I'm sorry, but are you aware you've asked an illegal question?"

Communication is another key element when you're a newly released prisoner looking for a job. It's not just about talking to your interviewer. You need to be able to get your message across to them.

Below are the factors that sum up good communication:

- 7% Spoken Words
- 38% Voice Tone, Pitch, Volume & Rate
- 55% Body Language
    - Posture
    - Clothing
    - Gestures
    - Facial Expressions

You want to do your best to positively communicate with your interviewer. If not, you may not even make it to the part where you get to explain your recent accomplishments.

Prepare a Felony Letter of Explanation

It's good to always be prepared. A Felony Letter of Explanation details the circumstances, time, nature and experience during and after serving time, from your perspective.

Remember, you need to sound as positive as possible. Below is an example of felony letter of explanation:

> **I was convicted of (Nature of the crime) ----------- in March of 2010. I served my sentence at (Name of the facility) -------------- for 12 months. During the course of my stay, I have had adequate time to reflect upon, consider and reconsider the actions that led me to sentence. I have realized things I ought to have done differently and would do**

differently if given another opportunity. My mistakes of the past and the consequences I suffered, afforded me the opportunity to better myself, mentally and psychologically.

During my incarceration period, I served as ----------- and got certified in -----------------. Since gaining my freedom I have worked in ----------- as ------------. I also volunteered my time at ---------------. In order to help me catch up and reintegrate, I also participated in a few re-entry programs. I'm looking for a full-time position in order to build a credible career in -----------------. I am optimistic that your organization is an ideal place for me to grow my career and further demonstrate the progress I have made so far.

I can understand your reluctance to hire any formerly incarcerated person. However, I'm eligible for the Federal Bonding program which protects you against any dishonesty or direct liability for me. Also, hiring me will make this organization eligible for Work Opportunity Tax Credit. I'd be glad to share more information about the above-mentioned programs upon request. My years of field experience in the area of ----------- make me a good fit for this position. I look forward to being afforded the opportunity to work for your prestigious company.

It's a case of different strokes for different folks when you're an ex-convict looking for a job on the outside. What works for one employer might not for another.

Skills and attributes one employer might find interesting and useful for the position you're aiming for may not be seen as the same to another.

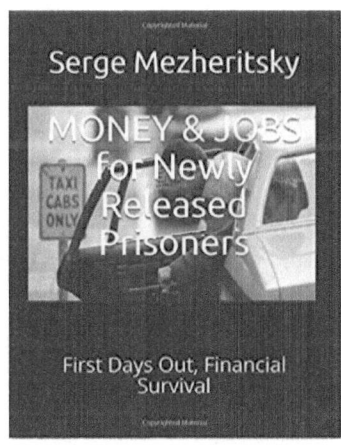

If you still need assistance finding a job after incarceration, check out the book **MONEY & JOBS for Newly Released Prisoners: First Days Out, Financial Survival** here: https://amzn.to/2JXF89j

Background Checks for Ex-Prisoners Looking for Jobs

Depending on the sophistication of the company and the role you're applying for, there are six basic background checks that can be run by a potential employer. The following may (and most likely will) be used to review your history:

1. Criminal record in the current state
2. Criminal records in all states
3. Federal criminal records
4. Credit checks
5. FBI File - This lets you know if you're currently under federal investigation too
6. Social Media Check - Largely done by using Google and popular social media platforms

Run a Criminal Background Check on Yourself Before the Interview

You should purchase a background check on yourself to find out what is on your record before potential employers see it. That way, you'll know what to expect during your next job interview.

Buy a background check from more than one company. Most of them get their results using different databases.

A popular loophole is most commercial databases only have federal prison sentences and not federal conviction records. This implies ex-convicts listed in these databases who served federal probation (and specifically served no time in a federal prison) may not be recorded in a commercial database.

In some cases, there are errors in the results, meaning you will need to have your criminal record corrected. Be sure to run your own background check as soon as possible just in case there are errors. The correction process will take time.

Get Your Credit Reports and Scores After Prison

Some employers run credit reports on potential candidates to determine how responsible they are in their personal lives. They use your credit scores and reports to help evaluate your overall character.

Your credit report can be obtained free every year from the three main credit reporting agencies:
1. Experian
2. Equifax
3. TransUnion

Your free reports can be accessed online at annualcreditreport.com.

You can also pay to access your credit scores online. That way, you know exactly what you're working with currently before any potential employers do.

Identity theft is another reason why you need to check your credit regularly. Ex-cons are often targets for identity theft because credit is left idle. While inside, there is generally no one to run your credit reports regularly for you during incarceration.

Family and friends, among numerous other possibilities, might have access to your social security number. Most identity thefts are perpetrated by people you actually know.

So, make sure you check your credit reports and scores as soon as you get out. That way, you know for sure that you're not a victim of identity fraud.

5 Job Opportunity Sources, Directories & Support Systems for Ex-Convicts

Resources and networking are very important tools for felons seeking jobs. Here are some support systems, directories and other resources to help you find a job after getting out of prison:

1. Non-Profit Organizations

Non-profit organizations are your best bet when it comes to finding the right support system to aid you during job hunting.

A few of these organizations have a restricted reach depending on their locations. Others have locations around the country.

2. Center for Employment Opportunities

The Center for Employment Opportunities (CEO) is a New York-based NGO (Non-Governmental Organization) with a wide reach all over the U.S. They provide immediate temporary transitional employment services for:

- Ex-cons on parole
- People on probation
- Sentenced inmates released by their local or county jails

CEO's long-term goal is to place the formerly incarcerated into permanent, unsubsidized full-time positions. They aim to find jobs that pay above minimum wage with solid benefits packages.

Program participants are put through interview and job-readiness training. CEO wants to integrate their participants into the labor market immediately. Other needed support services that are assessed and sometimes met include:

- Housing
- Clothing
- Childcare
- Documentation (IE, driver's license, social security card, birth certificate, etc...)

Get more info on CEO here: https://ceoworks.org

Participants in the ex-offender job program meet weekly with a designated employment specialist. Once CEO assists with a successful job placement, they monitor participants for up to one year.

3. Safer Foundation

Safer Foundation is one of the nation's largest community-based employment service providers for the formerly incarcerated. The Chicago-based organization provides re-entry and prison-based services to both ex-offenders in the U.S., especially in Chicago or the Quad City areas of Illinois and Iowa.

This foundation works in collaboration with the Illinois Department of Correction to give re-entry services to offenders housed at the Sheridan Correctional facility and two state ATCs (Adult Transition Centers).

Prisoners get education and life skills while still in custody. After their prison releases, their services include intensive job placement training and basic skills classes.

Once a client has been placed on a job, employment specialists monitor the employee through their employer for 30 days.

Get more info on Safer Foundation here: http://www.saferfoundation.org

4. Project RIO

Project RIO (Reintegration of Offenders) is a re-entry service program operated through Texas' state employment agency, the Texas Workforce Commission. This program is ideal for anyone in the state or planning to move there.

Participants are identified from state prison schools. Assessment specialists then consider the job market in the area prisoners will be released to, as well as the abilities of said prisoners. Major emphasis is placed on helping participants who don't have the documentation required for job-readiness.

All Project RIO participants go through life skills and employability training. The program is backed by a seven series workbook to help prepare ex-convicts prepare for their job searches.

Project RIO remains involved with its participant over the entire period of supervision. They diminish their involvement as the situation stabilizes for their formerly incarcerated participants.

After their participants land jobs, employment specialists contact their employers by phone at 30, 60 and 90-day intervals to see how things are going for them.

Get more info on Project RIO here: https://www.ncjrs.gov/pdffiles/168637.pdf

5. Other Agencies That Assist with Ex-Con Employment and/or Training

The following Non-Governmental Organizations can't directly employ everyone. But they can provide recommendations, free training and various other resources. They regularly have special jobs opportunities available to felons:

- The Work Place CA is a California based NGO: http://theworkplacegroup.ca
- Changing Lives Through Jobs (Chrysalis) is based in Southern California: https://changelives.org
- Goodwill operates everywhere in the United States and always helps the disadvantaged and disabled: http://www.goodwill.org
- United Way is an NGO based in Virginia with nationwide reach that offers various means of support for the less privileged and oppressed: https://www.unitedway.org
- Delancey Street Foundation is another NGO that helps ex-convicts and drug addicts which has offices in a number of states across the US: http://www.delanceystreetfoundation.org
- Career One Stop has nationwide coverage and assists with placement of ex-convicts as well in many states: https://www.careeronestop.org

If you ever face sexual or racial discrimination in the workplace and need legal help, contact The U.S. Legal Action Center at: http://www.lac.org

Government & Local Job Portals That Help Former Prisoners

Recent pressure from the Ban the Box campaign helped limit discrimination in the public civil service labor force. This campaign was designed to discourage unnecessary questions regarding a person's criminal history.

Now, most government job directories have a higher number of employment opportunities accommodating ex-cons. A few of the states have specially designed re-entry programs for ex-convicts.

We have compiled a list of official job portals for the U.S. federal government, all 50 state governments and Washington D.C.

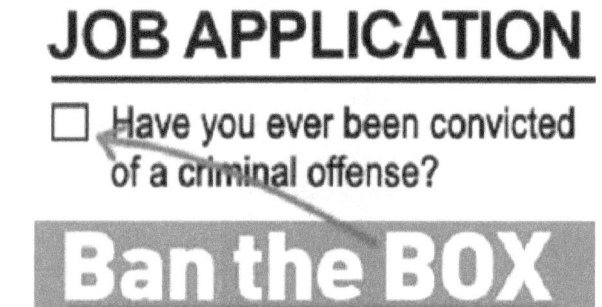

Learn more about Ban the Box here: https://bantheboxcampaign.org

Jobs for Ex-Convicts: Official Employment Portals for Each State in The U.S.

Searching for the right job after incarceration is far from an easy task. From false job advertisements to overly stringent job criteria, you have a lot to wade through.

All state governments in The U.S. have online job portals. They post openings in their civil service departments. Most government job portals allow hand-picked private employers to upload their job openings to these websites.

In some cases, the government has special portals for a re-entry plan. The Maryland Government Re-entry Program is one such case.

Below is a complete and up-to-date list of every government job portal in the U.S. It includes both links to the job portals of the federal government, all 50 states plus Washington D.C.

State Agency's Employment Portals

For ex-prisoners, government job portals are a great way to find opportunities that are more accommodating. Many of the job openings uploaded to these portals are civil service openings.

These employers can't discriminate against minorities. In a few cases, certain jobs consider the criminal records of applicants for understandable reasons.

Please visit us online for an interactive list of links to these job portals here: https://prisonrideshare.org/nonprofit/federal-state-agencies-help-former-prisoners-find-jobs/

Private Job Portals

The career portals of private companies and small businesses are good places to find job listings for ex-prisoners. However, there are no guarantees that a past criminal record wouldn't be a deciding factor in employment.

There are numerous openings where past offenses wouldn't be a problem. Many companies have a history of employing formerly incarcerated people. Some big companies that are known to hire felons include:

- UPS
- U-Haul
- Home Depot
- Amazon
- Denny's
- Walmart
- Costco
- Coca-Cola
- Target
- FedEx
- Best Buy
- Dropbox
- Facebook
- Gap
- Google
- Hershey
- Kroger

- LinkedIn
- Lyft
- PepsiCo
- Staples
- Starbucks
- Uber
- WeWork
- Xerox
- American Airlines

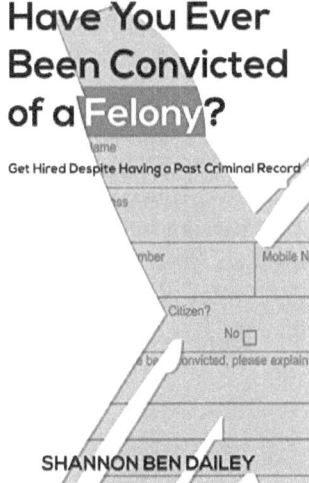

If you need more assistance, check out the book *Have You Ever Been Convicted of a Felony: Get Hired Despite Having a Past Criminal Record*.

Top 100 Employers Who Hire Ex-Prisoners in the U.S.

This is America. It's a capitalist economy, and every business wants to be on the profit end of things.

Businesses often make decisions devoid of sentiments and in the interest of their profits. How consumers perceive a company affects their profit bottom line. Therefore, it means a lot to them.

The public image of most companies is largely dependent upon:

- Company personnel
- Brand product or services
- Public relations

Many employers discriminate against ex-prisoners. They cite fallacious studies and public sentiments as the major reasons. So, don't be too expectant when applying for your next job interview. Be ready to face some felon discrimination.

At the same time however, don't let it stop you either.

Many progressive 21st century companies are finally coming around. They are more accommodating to the formerly incarcerated. A great number of these giant multinational companies have made it known that they do not care about a potential employee's criminal past.

As long as they are competent for the job, their qualifications will be the only deciding factors.

100 Jobs That Tend to Hire Felons

We have carefully researched all of the companies listed below. Through diligent research, we've verified that they have openings from time to time that don't restrict any qualified person from applying.

Below, we have listed the industry (niche) of each company and embedded a link to their respective job portals:

1. AAMCO (Auto maintenance)
2. ACE HARDWARE (Retail, Home improvement)
3. ALLIED VAN LINES (Moving Company)
4. AMERICAN GREETINGS (Greeting card)

5. ANDERSON WINDOWS (Manufacturing)
6. APPLE INC. (Computer hardware, Computer software, Consumer electronics, Digital distribution)
7. ARAMARK (Managed Services)
8. AT&T (Telecommunications)
9. AVON PRODUCTS (Personal care)
10. BASKIN-ROBBIN (Food and Beverage)
11. BED, BATH & BEYOND (Retail)
12. BLACK & DECKER (Power tools, home improvement products)
13. BLUE CROSS AND BLUE SHIELD ASSOCIATION (Health insurance)
14. BRAUM'S INC (Food, restaurants)
15. BRIDGESTONE (Auto and Truck parts)
16. BUFFALO WILD WINGS Restaurant
17. CAMPBELL'S SOUP (Food processing)
18. CANON (Electronics
19. CARL-S JR (Fast food)
20. CATERPILLAR INC. (Heavy equipment, Engines, Financial services)
21. CDW (Business to Business, Technology Infrastructure and Resale Services)
22. CHILI'S (Restaurant)
23. CHIPOTLE (Restaurants)
24. CINTAS Service
25. COMMUNITY EDUCATION CENTERS (Re-entry treatment, Education services)
26. CONAGRA FOODS (Food processing)
27. DAIRY QUEEN (Restaurants)
28. DELTA FAUCET (Home improvement)
29. DENNY'S (Restaurants)
30. DOLE FOOD COMPANY (Agribusiness)
31. DOLLAR RENT A CAR (Car rental)
32. DOLLAR TREE (Retail, Variety, Discount)
33. DR. PEPPER (Beverage)
34. DUNLOP TIRES (Automotive)
35. DUNKIN' DONUTS (Food and Beverage)
36. DUPONT (Chemicals)
37. DURACELL (Batteries)
38. EPSON (Electronics)
39. ERMCO, INC.(Electric)
40. FAMILY DOLLAR (Retail)
41. FIRESTONE COMPLETE AUTO CARE (Automotive)
42. PILOT FLYING J (Truckstop, Convenience store, Petroleum, Restaurant)

43. FRUIT OF THE LOOM (Clothing)
44. FUJIFILM (Consumer electronics)
45. GENERAL ELECTRIC (Conglomerate)
46. GENERAL MILLS Food processing
47. GEORGIA-PACIFIC (Pulp and paper)
48. GOODWILL (Job Finder)
49. GRAINGER (Industrial Supply Distribution)
50. GREYHOUND (Intercity bus transportation)
51. HANES (Clothing)
52. HILTON HOTELS (Hotels & Restaurants)
53. HOME DEPOT (Retail)
54. IBM (Computer hardware, Computer software, IT consulting)
55. IN-N-OUT BURGER (Restaurants)
56. JACK IN THE BOX (Fast food)
57. K-MART (Retail)
58. KELLY MOORE PAINTS (Paint manufacturing)
59. KFC (Restaurant)
60. KOHL'S (Retail)
61. KRAFT FOODS (Food processing)
62. KROGER (Retail)
63. LONGHORN STEAKHOUSE (Restaurant)
64. LOWE'S (Retail)
65. LSG SKY CHEFS (In-flight Service)
66. MCDONALD'S (Restaurant)
67. MEN'S WEARHOUSE (Retail)
68. METALS USA (Metal service)
69. MILLER BREWING COMPANY (Alcoholic beverage)
70. MOTOROLA (Telecommunications)
71. THE NEW YORK TIMES (Daily newspaper)
72. OLIVE GARDEN (Restaurant)
73. PEPSICO (Beverages, Chips)
74. PHILLIP MORRIS INC. (Tobacco)
75. PILGRIM'S (Food Products)
76. PRAXAIR (Chemicals)
77. RADISSON (Hotels)
78. RED LOBSTER (Restaurant)
79. RED ROBIN (Restaurant)
80. RESTAURANT DEPOT (Retail)
81. REYES BEVERAGE GROUP (Food service)
82. SAFEWAY (Retail)

83. TRADER JOES (Retail (grocery))
84. TYSON FOODS (Food processing)
85. U-HAUL (Rentals)
86. US STEEL CORPORATION (Steel)
87. VOLUNTEERS OF AMERICA (Nonprofit organization)
88. WALGREENS Retail
89. WENDY'S (Restaurant)
90. WINCO FOODS (Retail)
91. WYNDHAM HOTELS (Hotel)
92. SALVATION ARMY (International charitable organization)
93. SEARS (Retail)
94. SEASONS 52 (Restaurant)
95. SHELL OIL (Oil, energy)
96. SHOPRITE (Supermarket, Grocery)
97. SONY (Conglomerate)
98. SUBWAY (Restaurant)
99. XEROX (Document services, Digital imaging, IT services, IT consulting)
100. YARD HOUSE (Restaurant)

Looking for direct links to these employers? Visit us online for links to these employers here: https://prisonrideshare.org/nonprofit/100-jobs-that-tend-to-hire-felons-us

Entrepreneurship: Looking Beyond Paid Employment for Ex-Prisoners

Oftentimes, for no rational reason, society stereotypes ex-convicts when it comes to employment. Even in the face of evident competence, they are not hired or restricted to entry-level positions with no chances of advancements.

This menace is a great contributor to recidivism, as well as a gateway to the famous 'Rat Race' for ex-prisoners.

Entrepreneurship for Felons

'Be your own boss' is probably the most overused motivational line out there. We all know, it's easier said than done.

Everyone has ideas in their heads that could lead them to financial independence. Only a few people have the required resources to get them there. Some of the common stumbling blocks to becoming an entrepreneur include:

- Funding
- Logistics
- Expertise
- Environment

The simple truth about entrepreneurship is it largely boils down to a simple equation: **resources = money**.

4 Tips for Getting Resources to Start Your Own Business

Regardless of all the stumbling blocks surrounding entrepreneurship, it is still a great route to financial independence, even for ex-prison inmates. However, when it comes to resources, x-prisoners don't have as many options as non-felons have.

Here are four tips to help you come up with the resources you need to launch your own business as an entrepreneur:

1. Soft loans and credit facilities.

There's nothing soft about soft loans. Before committing to resources like this, be sure you're getting the money for a worthy cause. Most credit services discriminate against ex-convicts. Shamefully, some of these services are from the government.

2. Look close to you.

Friends and family are some of the best support and structure systems anyone could ever have. They have been there since the beginning. But, reaching out and asking for money is not as easy as it sounds.

It is even harder if you had a questionable reputation before serving time. There is no harm in trying though. If you get your act together and show them how serious you are, it may be the last time you need to ask for money... ever.

3. Earn to save, save to establish.

Menial and entry-level jobs can lead you to financial freedom with the right mentality. Use what you earn to start your own business. Before embarking on a paid job, decide how much you need to start your venture.

Regardless of how small your income is, you can set some of it aside to fuel your ambition. This way, you know how long you have to work until you can start your own business. The good thing about working before starting your own business is the field experience you will get.

It will benefit you as you run your own company. Even if you're not able to save all the money you need, the fact that you have something saved helps other people want to assist you.

4. Launch a Crowdfunding Campaign.

Another option to raise the required capital for your business is to start a fundraising campaign on an online crowdfunding platform. GoFundMe is just one of many web-based crowdfunding platforms. There are some offline too.

There are also investor crowdfunding platforms where people contribute money to your venture for a stake in your business. One important suggestion you should keep in mind when using crowdfunding as an option to raise funds: **Have a compelling story**.

Aim to write a pitch that sounds like a story you'd want to contribute to. If you accomplish that, you're bound to reel in some potential investors.

Entrepreneurship: Do Your Due Diligence First

Being an entrepreneur isn't an easy business venture at all. If you think it will give you the liberty to work when you feel like it and make you a billionaire soon, you must also keep in mind that you're solely responsible for any losses as well.

When starting your entrepreneurial venture, you need to have a solid business plan with all your contingencies in order, first and foremost. Furthermore, you must have (or employ) the required expertise in this field needed to run your business.

Lucrative Business Ideas for the Ex-Convict Entrepreneur

Every business can be profitable (some admittedly more than the others). But, with enough consistent hard work across the board, it is indeed possible. Here are a few business niche suggestions for ex-prisoners hoping to become business owners:

Service Areas

The American service industry is always a good place to look into. America pays good money for services after all. Programming and digital marketing are new and emerging service areas to be explored as well.

Depending on the scale you intend to launch your business, you may be required to have basic field knowledge or experience. Here are some of the services area suggestions for entrepreneurial opportunities:
- Tiling
- Barbers
- Painting
- Plumbers
- Carpentry
- Electricians
- Hairdressers
- Makeup artists
- Goldsmith
- Jeweler

Production Niches

This might be quite expensive to get into. You need to meet certain regulatory requirements. Often, you also need a special license. Your business will be subjected to more taxes as a result. In the short term, it will require more funding to start-up and a waiting period to turn a profit. It will take some time to yield well in this field.

In the production niche, there is also the problem of reaching your target market. The competition is quite stiff. In the long term, going into production of goods can be a lovely business.

The food business is one of the most popular for this reason. There are also cosmetics and body care products which are quite lucrative.

Freelance Gigs

The internet is without a doubt one of the best innovations for people in the 21st century. It can expose the world of opportunities, all with great ease of access. Freelancing is increasing in popularity for this reason.

There are high-in-demand skills needed to fetch a good income online. Some freelance gigs great for people who have served prison time involving these skills include:

- Professional Blogging
- Programming
- Content Writing
- Graphics Designing
- Virtual Assisting
- Digital Marketing
- Website Administrator
- Database Management
- Create Videos for Others

There are online tutorials and resources where you can learn these skills. They are readily available on YouTube and affordable on Udemy.

Entrepreneurship Isn't for All Former Prisoners

Don't be ashamed to admit that entrepreneurship isn't for you at some point. You are taking a risk as an entrepreneur while managing most aspects of your own business. As such, it's important to remember that an excellent team member doesn't always make an excellent team leader.

Part of managing your own business is human resources. People are not the easiest to manage. But, it's not always easy doing everything yourself. If hiring employees seems like too much in the beginning, try using freelancers instead.

If you are not sure about your qualifications as an entrepreneur, but you have the burning desire to be your own boss, give it a try. It might not be a bad idea after all.

How to Get Credit for Your Business as an Ex-Convict

After paying their debts to society, most felons find it difficult to generate steady incomes. According to a study published by the Bureau of Justice, it is reported that only 12.5% of labor employers will consider (which may never lead to hiring) a job application from an ex-convict.

Reference: https://news.wbhm.org/feature/2014/life-after-prison-ex-felons-often-struggle-to-find-a-job

Another bottleneck aiding these stereotypes is the legal limit of where certain ex-felons can work. Depending on the nature of the crime committed, an ex-felon may be disqualified from certain job types.

Jobs like child care, female care, pharmaceuticals, medicals, armed forces or anything involving the handling of money are some of the most popular jobs restricted from ex-convicts. These determents are what lead many felons to become entrepreneurs.

Looking for more ideas for launching your own business after incarceration? Check out the book entitled **Fresh Startup: 8 Businesses Felons Can Start Right Out Of Prison** for assistance here: https://amzn.to/2Dz4KsP

Top 10 Avenues to Get Small Business Grants for the Formerly Incarcerated

Starting a business is a good idea for anyone looking to start all over. It offers a good chance at financial independence and saves you the corporate drama. However, the reality of limited resources (largely financial) makes it harder to progress with independent business launches.

Unfortunately, just like corporate employers do, most loan, grant or credit-granting services discriminate against ex-prisoners. Only a few platforms are welcoming and have a track record of giving grants to people who have done prison time.

Below are 10 avenues to get credit if you're looking to start your own business as an ex-convict:

1. Correctional Facilities

Most correctional facilities run or partner with programs that train inmates in job skills. A good number of these prison job training programs contain services which are empowering enough to start a small-scale business.

Don't underestimate such services, as there aren't many genuine options for you. For example, you may be taught how to use Microsoft Office tools. In that case, laptops may be handed out alongside a premium version of the latest state-of-the-art software.

These are things that can easily cost you up $1,000 or more if you were to get them yourself without these services.

2. Inmates to Entrepreneurs

Inmates to Entrepreneurs is funded by Sageworks. It's meant to empower formerly incarcerated people. They do this by getting them the right information required to:

- Start over
- Establish their own businesses
- Become economically productive citizens

Networking is a big thing in organizations like this. Attending their online and in-person seminars is beneficial in gaining the knowledge and skills required to do independent business. You'll also meet the right people and find effective platforms to help you launch your company.

Inmate to Entrepreneurs is a nonprofit community outreach organization found here: https://inmatestoentrepreneurs.org

3. Helpforfelons.org

This website is a platform that focuses on everything related to re-entry. From helpful materials to directories and personnel, this site is a deep, informative resource that will make things easy for any formerly incarcerated person.

Helpforfelons.org aren't likely to directly give grants or loans. Yet, they can be instrumental in connecting you to platforms where you can get such. Check out this page on their website for links to all state programs assisting felons with re-entry: https://helpforfelons.org

4. Federal Education Loans

In pursuit of your ambition to establish your own business, you may need to learn certain skills. Graphics design, web design, accounting and HVAC technicians are some of the popular certifications that can be required in starting a business.

Getting the training necessary for these certified skills can be expensive. That's why Federal Education Loans have become a go-to source for funding new business ventures.

Being a formerly incarcerated person doesn't disqualify anyone from the Federal Student Loan or Federal Pell Grant. You can obtain a federal loan to learn the skills you require to launch your company.

More information on Federal Education Loans: https://studentaid.ed.gov/sa/types/loans

For information about eligibility for these Federal Education Loans, check out grants.gov and search through all federal government grant services here: https://www.grants.gov

5. SBA Microloans

In general, it's not easy to get a loan from SBA (Small Business Association), especially for a startup. This is due to the stringent measures put in place to scrutinize the viability and sustainability of businesses to which they give loans.

An SBA Microloan is your best chance at getting anything. The microloan focuses on business loan requests under $50,000 with $13,000 as the average amount this service grants.

The SBA doesn't make or give loans directly. Instead, they work with approved lenders and guarantee a good portion of the loan.

Get more info on SBA Microloans here: https://www.sba.gov/blogs/financing-your-small-business-microloan

6. Federal Trade Commission (FTC)

The 'be your own boss' wave is sweeping a lot of candidates, and scammers are taking advantage of that. These days, the internet is awash with con-artists preying on financially desperate innocents.

It's easy to find promises of earning income from stuffing envelopes, telemarketing or medical billing from the comfort of your couch.

Before sending money to any of these schemes or signing any contract, visit the FTC website and follow their advice on detecting scams here: https://www.ftc.gov

The rule of thumb when it comes to detecting fraud is *'look before you leap, if it sounds too good to be true, be careful and look again'.*

7. Crowdfunding Campaigns

Sites like GoFundMe.com and IndieGoGo.com have collectively raised up to $10 billion for individuals and their projects in the last 10 years. The best thing about crowdfunding is that nobody cares whether you've ever been incarcerated or not.

GoFundMe is a personal finance raising platform where you freely create campaigns. Donors feel comfortable giving to reputable crowdfunding websites like this one.

Your only job here is to **create a convincing crowdfunding campaign** that would compel even you to give yourself money. From education to medical expense and business, lay a compelling case for the GoFundMe community. You're bound to get some investors.

IndieGoGo is more prolific for funding new inventions or product ideas. If you have a unique idea or product, you can get support and funding from experts and innovation enthusiasts by launching and managing your project. The crowdfunding platform can connect you with partners in the areas of product design, distribution, even prototyping.

There are numerous other crowdfunding websites. But the above mentioned are the most prolific and proven of them all. Your ability to create a compelling campaign while also promoting the campaign beyond their platform will go a long way in assisting you to reach your target.

8. SBDC (Small Business Development Centers)

SBDC is a nationwide nonprofit network. The association of Small Business Development Centers aids existing businesses as well as startups. They usually tailor their services in partnership with universities and colleges in particular locations.

Today, SBDC offers benefits such as free advice, counseling and business consultations from attorneys, marketing and accounting experts, among others. The company also hosts seminars, symposiums and networking events to help people grow and start their own small businesses.

Get more info on SBDC here: https://americassbdc.org

9. Freelance Marketplaces

Starting a skill-based online business can give you a lot of leverage in this day and age. Aside from the fact that it doesn't cost much to set up, running the business is also easy.

Freelance marketplaces can serve as an incubation ground for your business. There are numerous high-demand skills trending in many freelance websites. These skills include graphic design, web design, content writing, marketing and knowledge sharing, just to name a few.

Upwork.com, Fiverr.com and Freelancer.com are three of the most popular freelance marketplaces. These sites match freelancers with independent contractors. Escrow payments are usually adopted to ensure transparency.

Rather than trying to look for your own clients, these freelance platforms have a ready pool of willing clients just waiting for you. In most cases, setting up your profile is all that needs to be done on your end.

If you are also looking to raise funds to embark on other ventures, freelancing can be your best bet. It keeps you staffed, while dodging the costs of hiring employees.

10. Your Community

A majority of the programs designed to support felons in starting their own businesses are locally-based and small. Don't be keen on farfetched help. Look within. The following offline and web resources can help you find government and private programs around you:

- State government offices/websites
- Federal government offices/websites
- Local county, district or government offices/websites
- Churches, mosques, temples and other religious organizations

These are great places to start when seeking credit services and facilities to start your business as an ex-convict.

Also noteworthy is that there are more grants and credits for nonprofit ideas than there are for profit businesses. To this effect, you may want to consider starting a nonprofit or redesigning your business model to be a non-profit social venture.

Get Help Establishing Personal Credit

If want to go far in life after being released from prison, credit will soon become an issue. You may want to finance a car, or even buy a home/ Many jobs use credit reports to make hiring decisions. And, if you plan to start your own business, good credit may be required to get the funding you need.

Therefore, having good credit will be essential to your long-term success on the streets. Even if you don't have bad credit, having a mentor to help you establish credit could make the process easier.

We have partnered with one of the top credit repair companies in the nation to create **Credit Repair Solutions for Ex-Inmates**. This is a special program designed specifically to help establish good credit after getting out of prison.

NOTE: This offer is not valid in GA, KS, LA, SC or VT.

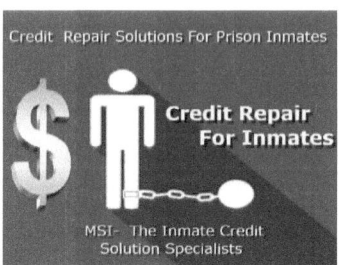

Ready to take the leap to having a high FICO score?
Go here for a FREE ex-inmate credit building consultation: http://bit.ly/2AJN9Np

Get Help Establishing Business Credit

Once you launch your own business, it's important to monitor its credit regularly. Just like with personal credit, scammers can create chaos that could take you years to fix.

So, it's wise to monitor your business credit activity before issues arise. This allows you to identify, early on, any potential risks that exist. You can also monitor your company's credit in one place. That way, you can:

- Adjust payment terms
- Branch out your streams of revenue
- Find new vendors
- Engage with potential partners

A business credit monitoring service gives you notice every time there's a change. Get notifications in real-time whenever someone runs your business credit report.

We have partnered with Equifax Small Business to help you not only monitor your company's credit but establish it as well. Get Peace of Mind with Equifax Small Business Credit Monitoring from true industry leaders.

Go here for details on Equifax Business Credit: http://bit.ly/2Q8Oepb

About Prison Rideshare Network

Prison Rideshare Network Corporation is a nonprofit organization dedicated to helping people visit their loved ones in prisons. This is done through a network of prison visitor transportation companies and prison loved ones who prefer carpooling to correctional facilities.

Our network members have been engaging through us since 2011 through our website and social media channels. Today, the process continues through our innovative PrisonLift app. This state-of-the-art web and mobile app puts finding businesses that give rides to facilities and prison carpool partners right at your fingers.

Stay in touch with us to keep up-to-date on prison news, PrisonLift app updates, tips and tools for prison loved ones and people who visit correctional institutions. Follow our blogs and you'll get discounts on prison visitor goods and custom gear for loved ones!

Engage with Us Online

PrisonLift - https://prisonrideshare.org/prisonlift

Prison News - https://prisonrideshare.org

Prison Loved Ones Blog - https://prisonrideshare.org/nonprofit/blog

Prison Fashion & Travel Blog - https://prisonrideshare.org/shop/blog

Prison Loved Ones & Visitors Store - https://prisonrideshare.org/shop

Facebook - https://facebook.com/PrisonRideshareNetwork

Twitter - https://twitter.com/prisonrideshare

Google+ - https://www.google.com/+PrisonrideshareOrgUSA

Instagram - http://instagram.com/prisonridesharenetwork

Pinterest - https://www.pinterest.com/prisonrideshare

LinkedIn - https://www.linkedin.com/in/prison-rideshare-network-a43b4529

YouTube - https://www.youtube.com/channel/UCwd0P8QVb30dqcg_K8cj-bw

Vimeo - https://vimeo.com/prisonridesharenetwork

This page has been left blank intentionally.

www.ingramcontent.com/pod-product-compliance
Lightning Source LLC
Chambersburg PA
CBHW030510220526
45464CB00006B/2740